SOUTH NORFOLK

VIRGINIA

1661–2005

Best wishes
to a fellow South Norfolk
citizens.

Raymond L. Harper

SOUTH NORFOLK VIRGINIA

1661–2005

VOLUME THREE

A VISUAL HISTORY

RAYMOND L. HARPER

Charleston · London

History
PRESS

Published by The History Press

Charleston, SC 29403

www.historypress.net

Front cover: It was 1:30 p.m. on November 11, 1949, when this Armistice Day parade got underway. The Boy Scouts of America were well represented. When this picture was taken the troop was passing the Portlock Elementary School. One corner of the high school building can be seen in the upper right corner; also there is a new 1949 Ford parked at the foot of the fire escape. *From the author's collection.*

Back cover: This picture, which was taken from the second floor of the South Norfolk municipal building in 1954, shows a busy part of what was known as downtown South Norfolk. The entrance to the overpass and the stores in Lane's Row can be seen on the left. Monroe's drug store is slightly right of center. The bus in the picture is heading north along Liberty Street. There are several signs and a birdbath on the lawn straight ahead from the municipal building. The signs were usually military recruiting posters. *Courtesy of Sargeant Memorial Room, Norfolk Public Library, Norfolk, Virginia.*

First published 2006

Manufactured in the United Kingdom

ISBN 1.59629.123.0

Library of Congress Cataloging-in-Publication Data

Harper, Raymond L.
    South Norfolk, Virginia (1661-2005) : a definitive history / by
Raymond L. Harper.
      p. ; cm.
    Includes bibliographical references and indexes.
    ISBN 1-59629-065-X (v. 1 : alk. paper) -- ISBN 1-59629-066-8
(v. 2 : alk. paper)
    1. South Norfolk (Chesapeake, Va.)--History. 2. Chesapeake
(Va.)--History.   I. Title.
  F234.C49H374 2005
  975.5'523--dc22

2005023473

CONTENTS

Acknowledgements   7
Introduction   9
An Overview of Local History   13

The 1800s   15
1900–1919   22
The 1920s   29
The 1930s   35
The 1940s   48
The 1950s   69
The 1960s   92
The 1970s–2005   99
Berkley—Village and Town   109

Other Books by the Author   123

ACKNOWLEDGEMENTS

I would first like to say that this third volume of my definitive history of South Norfolk will live in my heart for the rest of my life. On March 7, 2006, the manuscript, 170 original vintage images along with their captions, hard copies and disks were complete and shipped. More than a week passed and the package had not arrived at the publisher. It was lost in shipment and at this time still has not been found. My choices were either forget volume III entirely or start over from the beginning. I chose the latter. When friends and acquaintances learned of my dilemma they came to my rescue. Both my phone and doorbell began to ring. People showed up with photographs that even I did not know existed. I am deeply indebted to these folks, for without them this volume would not be possible.

I would like to express my sincere appreciation to the many individuals who supplied me with photographs and other information used in this book. I would especially like to thank Kaye Herndon, who furnished rare photographs of Dr. and Mrs. George N. Halstead, Dr. Nick Wilson and other members of the Wilson family. To Stuart Smith, who always shares his picture postcards and other information with me, I am truly grateful. My thanks to Robert Hitchings and Troy Valos; Kirn Memorial Library—City of Norfolk, Virginia; Anne Howell Maheu, who provided me with her father's collection of photographs of the South Norfolk Panthers and the Aces and other early South Norfolk photographs; Frankie Sweetwood, who donated her large collection of photographs taken throughout the years at the Texas Oil Company terminal along the Southern Branch of the Elizabeth River in South Norfolk; to Hunter Joyce Burt, daughter of James Justin Joyce, president of Reliance Fertilizer and Lime Corporation, who furnished a picture of her father's plant at the end of Barnes Road across from the Jordan Bridge; Charles Hackworth, of Hackworth Reprographics Inc., who so graciously furnished me with reduced copies of large images; to J. James Davis Jr., son of Mayor J. James Davis, who provided me with photographs and information from his father's long and successful political career; Bennie White Jr.; Susan Curling Watts; William Elliott; Lois Wood; Lou Trzinski; Richard Spratley; Hardy Forbes; Mildred Gay; Burnie Mansfield; N. Duval Flora, retired treasurer of both South Norfolk and Chesapeake; Charles A. (Dick) Harrell; and Ben White, with the City of Chesapeake Economic Development Department.

I would like to dedicate this book to my wife Emma Lee Rock Harper. Thank you for fifty-seven wonderful years. Also to our two daughters, Shari and Karen, and to our three grandchildren, Alexa Raye, Colby John and Colin Steven Rudis.

INTRODUCTION

When you mention South Norfolk, many of today's citizens ask if it was ever a part of the City of Norfolk. The answer to that question is a most definite no. During my tour of duty with the United States Navy I was sometimes asked the name of my hometown. Upon answering that I was from South Norfolk, Virginia, someone would say, "Oh! You're from Sh—— City." My reply was always, "No, that's the city across the river."

South Norfolk, like all the other nearby communities, was once a part of Norfolk County. As it has been stated in several of my other books, South Norfolk had its beginning in 1661 when the third chapel of the Elizabeth River Parish was built on land between Jones Creek and Scuffletown Creek in the vicinity of present-day Lakeside Park and Barnes Road.

Throughout the colonial period and most of the nineteenth century the area was like its neighboring rural sections in that it followed the agricultural way of life. It was not until after the Civil War ended in 1865, rail service was resumed in 1866 and the outside influences (the Yankees) were removed in 1870 that the real industrial potential of the area began to be realized. By the end of the first decade of the twentieth century there were seventy-one industrial plants along the Southern Branch of the Elizabeth River in or near the South Norfolk area.

Many of the streets had already received their names from the Poindexter family, which had come to the area before the Civil War. Reginald Poindexter has been credited with having given the name "South Norfolk" to the community prior to 1890. A study of the War of 1812 reveals that most of the early streets were named for famous sea captains who had fought in the war. Guerriere Street, however, was named for the HMS *Guerriere*, which was captured by Captain Isaac Hull and the crew of the USS *Constitution* during the War of 1812.

By the latter 1800s and early 1900s, men who had been active in the development of Berkley had built several handsome homes in South Norfolk. Among them were E.M. Tilley, John Jones, Foster Black, William Sloane, Thomas Woodard, J.P. Andre' Mottu and George Grimes. These men and possibly others built homes in the young community south of Berkley. South Norfolk began to grow rapidly by the development of ten different tracts of land.

In 1873 J. Alonzo McCloud operated the only store. At that time the community was known as McCloudtown. By 1888 Sam W. Wilson's grocery business was situated in a small frame house on Liberty Street near the Norfolk and Western Railway crossing. At that time Wilson's investment amounted to just fifty dollars.

Around 1900 and 1901 a number of other businesses opened in South Norfolk. On Liberty Street were retail businesses such as confectioners, dry goods merchants, a laundry, an eating house, a fish and oyster dealer, a furniture dealer, and a saloon.

Contributing largely to the growth and development of the community was the extension of the Berkley Street Railway from the limits of Berkley to a point at the intersection of Chesapeake Avenue and Guerriere Street. At a later date the streetcar line was extended to the limits of South Norfolk and on to the industrial area of Money Point.

By this time there were two churches in the community. The Liberty Street Methodist Episcopal Church, South, had been dedicated in May 1892 and the South Norfolk Baptist Church followed with a formal dedication on June 11, 1893. Also, by 1891, South Norfolk's first public school had been built in what would become the 1100 block of Jackson Street and Miss Rena B. Wright was its principal.

The wooden two-room school on Jackson Street soon became inadequate for the growing student population. Around the turn of the century the Washington District School Board purchased a block of land on B Street in Elmsley between Twentieth and Twenty-second Streets and built a new school that opened at the beginning of the school year in 1902. A second building would be ready for use in 1910 and a third in 1916.

In September 1934, my mother escorted me to the school on B Street and enrolled me in the first grade. My teacher was a tiny but powerful lady by the name of Shanah Pulliam. Miss Pulliam had taught my older brother, Jesse, and my father, and possibly my grandfather. I would go on to receive my elementary and secondary education from the South Norfolk public schools.

During my youth, Chesapeake Avenue was considered the elite section of the city. It was the location of many large homes that had been built around the turn of the century. Beautiful tall trees lined both sides of the street, meeting in the center to form an arch that produced shade from spring until late fall of each year. Today this is part of the South Norfolk Historic District.

Everything was within walking distance and wherever you went you were met by friends. World War II saw many people come to the area to work in the shipyards and other defense industries. These new citizens seemed to fit right in. After the war some stayed and made South Norfolk their permanent home while others decided to return to their prewar roots.

In those days, when you heard the word "drug" it was usually in reference to the local drug stores where young people met to talk and sip soft drinks and milkshakes. In those days, parents were not faced with juvenile drug use and other problems like the parents of today.

In 1963, the local political scene changed and the members of city council felt that merging with Norfolk County would lead to bigger and better things. This did not happen, for the tax dollars collected from South Norfolk were not used in the former city. As a result, what was once a thriving city began to deteriorate, unsavory characters moved in and the area began to decay. Most of the original families moved out and many of the fine old homes were used by new owners as rental properties. Rent was collected but very little upkeep was accomplished. Now it seems things are beginning to turn around. Young families that are interested in historic restoration are purchasing and restoring some of the original beautiful old homes. It would be nice if the streetcars could return.

This volume consists of historic images to accompany volumes I and II of the definitive history of South Norfolk published in 2005. It is my intent to use a large number of photographs that have not appeared in my other books. Here you will find images dating from the 1800s to 2005. I hope you enjoy them.

So settle back and join me in a trip down memory lane and while we are at it, let's have a look at a few recent happenings.

An Overview of Local History

It was on April 10, 1606, that King James authorized the creation of two companies to settle Virginia (which has been defined as the 34th and 45th degrees of north latitude—from Cape Fear River in North Carolina to Passamaquoddy Bay in Maine). The London Company would settle the southern region and the Plymouth Company, the northern region.

One year later, on May 13, 1607, representatives of the London Company and their settlers began a settlement on the river they named James at a place they called Jamestown. (The four hundredth anniversary of Jamestown will be celebrated in 2007.)

On November 18, 1618, with the number of settlements and settlers in the region along the Chesapeake Bay and the James River having increased so much, the Virginia Company's London Council ordered that the Virginia colony be divided into four large corporations. For purposes of local administration each was to be a parish of the Church of England. Sir George Yeardley was appointed governor and the county-parish system of government began. A bicameral legislative assembly was established with representatives from each of the corporations.

Between the years 1632 and 1634, the Virginia colony was divided into eight shires, or counties. The original shires were Accawmack (now Accomack), Charles City, Charles River (later York County), Elizabeth City, Henrico, James City, Warrosquyoake (later Isle of Wight) and Warwick River. In 1636, the County of New Norfolk, that area south of the James River and Hampton Roads, was partitioned from Elizabeth City County.

In 1637, the county of New Norfolk was subdivided into Upper Norfolk County (formerly Nansemond County, now the City of Suffolk) and Lower Norfolk County. In 1691, Lower Norfolk County was divided into Norfolk County and Princess Anne County. It was in 1705 that Norfolk was established as a town and port. Thirty-one years later, in 1736, the Borough of Norfolk was formed.

In 1752 the Town of Portsmouth was created on land owned by Colonel Crawford and in 1845 the City of Norfolk was partitioned from Norfolk County. Likewise, in 1858, the Town of Portsmouth became a city.

On September 19, 1919, the village of South Norfolk was incorporated as a town, and on January 5, 1921, it became a city of the second class. After annexing the town of Portlock, South Norfolk met the requirements to become a city of the first class and this was accomplished in 1951.

On January 1, 1963, what remained of Norfolk County merged with the City of South Norfolk to become the City of Chesapeake.

THE 1800s

As stated before, the area that became South Norfolk experienced a small amount of settlement during the colonial period but remained rural until the late nineteenth century. The City of Norfolk, located across the Eastern Branch of the Elizabeth River, did not reach its full potential until after the post–Civil War depression, when railroads began to bring coal and produce from the west and south. The new railroads were a boon to Norfolk and also to the farms and villages of Norfolk County. Norfolk's location on the Elizabeth River gave it a prime position for shipping, but prohibited a natural expansion across the river's Eastern Branch. When the railroads came through Norfolk County, they encouraged development all along the line. New industries grew up along the Eastern and Southern Branches of the Elizabeth River and new businesses and houses appeared near the railroad lines.

Prior to 1870, the entire south side was referred to as Berkley or that land near or south of Norfolk. Although several houses had been built in the area, some businessmen began to make plans for development of South Norfolk as early as 1889.

The farm comprising the land between Berkley and what is now Poindexter Street was known as the Green House Tract. Alvah H. Martin and others purchased this property, divided it into lots and put them on the market under the name of Elmsley. In 1890 Martin and his wife donated two of those lots for construction of the first church in South Norfolk. The church, which was given the name Liberty Street Methodist Episcopal Church, South, was dedicated in May 1892. The South Norfolk Baptist Church, which began as a chapel on January 5, 1893, was the second house of worship in South Norfolk.

The first store in the area was that of J. Alonza McCloud and it opened in 1873. In 1888, Sam W. Wilson began his grocery and feed store in a small frame house on Liberty Street. Wilson eventually purchased McCloud's store and the business remained in operation for about seventy years.

The Chesapeake Knitting Mill was built near the dividing line between Berkley and South Norfolk in 1890. The mill was built by David Lowenberg and leased by Foster Black who, along with his young nephew William Sloane, had come from New York in 1887. South Norfolk's Lowenberg Mill, which was later named the Elizabeth Knitting Mill, was built in 1892. Both mills furnished employment to a large number of Berkley and South Norfolk residents.

The earliest family records are those of the Portlocks. Although records show that John Portlock first visited the area in 1685, it is believed that the earliest representative of the family came from England around 1634. The family settled in what became known as Portlock Estates in the vicinity of Norfolk. This property would not become a part of South Norfolk until 1951.

Among the early settlers of the South Norfolk area were Admiral Carter W. Poindexter and his family. Poindexter originally built his home, called the Anchorage, on the waterfront across from the Gosport Navy Yard. Later the family moved from the waterfront to a house on Ohio Street in what is now the 1000 block. When the Poindexters left Ohio Street, they relocated to a house that J.P. Andre' Mottu had built on his property in the vicinity of what is today the corner of Rodgers and Jefferson Streets.

Among the other South Norfolk homes that were built in the 1800s was that of John Jones. Jones, a building contractor, built his house at what is now 1130 Chesapeake Avenue around 1888. He began construction of his father-in-law, Edward Munro Tilley's home in 1890 and completed it in 1893. Tilley's home, which included twenty-two rooms and seven fireplaces, still stands today at the corner of Chesapeake Avenue and Guerriere Street. The home is sometimes referred to as the Tilley mansion. E.M. Tilley had two other large homes built around this time. The one diagonally across from his at 1049 Chesapeake Avenue was the home of his son George Thomas Tilley. The other large and impressive house built at 17 Ohio Street was the home of his other son, William Munro Tilley. Frank Livingston Portlock Sr. purchased this house in 1910.

Two other early homes were built on Poindexter Street in what is now the 1400 block. Captain George Funk built his house in 1894. Across the street was the home of George L. Grimes. Grimes married Anna Eliza Hockaday on June 21, 1888, in Berkley and moved into his home on Poindexter Street soon after the wedding.

In the spring of 1892, Nicholas George Wilson began the study of medicine under his uncle (by marriage), Edward W. Mumma. The following September, Nick entered the medical department of the University of Maryland in Baltimore. In 1895, he graduated with the degree of doctor of medicine and in June of the same year he passed the Virginia State Board of Medical Examiners. He began the practice of general medicine at the home of his Aunt Carrie Edwards on Liberty Street Extended in South Norfolk.

On November 28, 1895, Dr. N.G. (Nick) Wilson married Beulah Halstead, the daughter of Dr. George Nolley Halstead. They resided in a small white house, which was surrounded by a white picket fence. The corner on which this house was built later became 1401 Poindexter Street and was known as Wilson's corner.

In 1898, Frank Sheppard Royster from Tarboro, North Carolina, built a large fertilizer plant in South Norfolk. On August 2, 1900, he changed the name to F.S. Royster Guano Company.

George Nolley Halstead attended the Norfolk County Public School until reaching the age of sixteen. At that time he entered the Virginia Collegiate Institute in Portsmouth, Virginia. In 1859, at the age of nineteen, he began reading medicine under Dr. W.J. Moore in Norfolk, Virginia. In October 1860, he entered the medical department of the University of Pennsylvania. The outbreak of the War Between the States led to the interruption of his medical studies at the university.

On April 20, 1861, Halstead enlisted as a private in Company I, Fifteenth Virginia Calvary. During the winter of 1862, he left the command to attend the Medical College of Virginia, completing his studies and graduating in March 1863. On July 15, 1863, he was commissioned assistant surgeon in the Confederate States (CS) Navy and received orders to the Naval Hospital in Richmond, Virginia. After this, Dr. Halstead saw eighteen months of ironclad duty. The war officially ended on Palm Sunday, April 9, 1865. Everyone was paroled and headed for home. Halstead reached home ten days later on April 19, 1865. *Photo courtesy of Kaye R. Herndon.*

It was on June 11, 1865, that Dr. George N. Halstead met Margaret Courtney Jane Wilson. It was love at first sight and they were married December 14, 1865, in Currituck County, North Carolina. This photograph was taken on their wedding day. *Photo courtesy of Kaye R. Herndon.*

This ca. 1892 photograph was taken on what is now Liberty Street. The horse standing on the boardwalk pulled the Berkley Express between the town of Berkley and the village of South Norfolk. The church in the left background at the corner of what became Twenty-second and Liberty Streets is the Liberty Street Methodist Episcopal Church, South. *Photo courtesy of Richard Womack.*

This house in the 1100 block of Jackson Street was built around 1898, and was the home of James Madison Eley. Eley had served as a private in Company F of the Sixty-first Virginia Regiment during the Civil War. James is the man in the yard with a hoe in his hand. He appears to be working his garden. His wife Mary is on the porch with three other ladies and one baby. The identity of the man with his foot on the fence rail is unknown. The house still stands today. *Photo courtesy of Jean Cooper.*

This unique image of the Norfolk and Portsmouth Belt Line Railroad Bridge across the Southern Branch of the Elizabeth River, which was built in 1897–98, shows a coal-fed locomotive pulling several boxcars. The bridge tender's station can be seen near the top of the structure. *Photo courtesy of Richard Spratley.*

In this photo we see a coal-fed locomotive pulling a caboose and several boxcars across the Norfolk and Portsmouth swing bridge. This image is reminiscent of a Lionel model at Christmastime. *Photo courtesy of Richard Spratley.*

This distinguished looking gentleman is John Cuthrell who, throughout his lifetime, operated several businesses of great importance in South Norfolk. Among them were a feed and grain store and an ice plant. He was also the founder of the Bank of South Norfolk, which later became the Merchant and Planters Bank and is today the Bank of America. Cuthrell built his home on Rodgers Street at the corner of Ohio Street in 1903. In 1939 his heirs sold this large three-story house to Francis and Mildred Gay who operated it as a funeral home. The home is now under the ownership Sid Oman and his son Robert. *Photo courtesy of J. James Davis Jr.*

This lovely lady, Sarah Elizabeth Cuthrell, was the wife of John Cuthrell. Sarah was born July 14, 1866, and died January 9, 1923. She and her husband John were laid to rest in Magnolia Cemetery in the Berkley section of Norfolk. *Photo courtesy of J. James Davis Jr.*

1900–1919

Around 1900 and 1901, there were a number of businesses in South Norfolk. Many of them were on Liberty Street. John Jackson, a physician, lived at what would later become 1041 Chesapeake Avenue. His carriage house was behind the main residence and near Seaboard Avenue. The Berkley Street Railway Company had its offices at the corner of Avenue C and Thirteenth Street. Miss Rena B. Wright was principal of the South Norfolk Public School on Jackson Street, the Reverend Paul Bradley was pastor of the Methodist Church and Samuel Robinson was minister of the South Norfolk Baptist Church. At this early date some industry was already moving into South Norfolk.

After the death of Foster Black in 1903, William Sloane, his nephew, ran both the Chesapeake and the Elizabeth Knitting Mills. Upon coming to the area in 1887, Sloane resided in Berkley. He married Florence Knapp in 1895 and they built their home on the corner of Chesapeake Avenue and Ohio Street in South Norfolk. This lovely old home still stands at 1203 Chesapeake Avenue.

By 1902, a thriving community existed where farms and strawberry fields had been just a few years earlier. The estimated population of South Norfolk was two thousand. It was in that year that Joseph Herbert Norton, who lived on Chesapeake Avenue, opened the Shirtwaist Factory on Poindexter Street. The factory opened in August and employed about one hundred people.

In 1904, Dr. Nicholas Wilson had a large handsome house built at 13 Chesapeake Avenue. In the early 1900s, W. Dean Preston built a large home on D Street at the corner of Twenty-second Street and in 1907, Sam Wilson built his new home on a triangular lot at the intersection of D and Decatur Streets. The back of the house faced Buchanan Street. Of these three the only one standing today is the house built by Sam Wilson.

By 1910, the Pocomont Guano Company and A.S. Lee and Sons, a lime manufacturing firm established by Arthur S. Lee of Richmond, Virginia, were operating on the waterfront. By May 1913, there were seventy-one industrial plants along the Southern Branch of the Elizabeth River either in or near South Norfolk.

In 1911, the magistrate's office was located in the Flatiron Building on Liberty Street near the Belt Line Railroad. Parke L. Poindexter was justice of the peace, C.P. Rogers was constable and E.H. Whitehurst was the chief of police. The Washington District of Norfolk County employed these men. Whitehurst lived at 64 Chesapeake Avenue.

The number of houses continued to increase in South Norfolk. More houses appeared on Chesapeake Avenue and on scattered lots throughout the southern section of the community. It was around 1914 that Dr. Frank Wilson purchased the home at 13 Chesapeake Avenue from his half brother Dr. Nick Wilson. Frank remained there until January 1919. He then sold it to J.R. Williams, who moved his funeral business from Chestnut Street in Berkley to the large house on Chesapeake Avenue in South Norfolk.

In 1915, the volunteer firemen built a new two-story fire station on Twenty-second Street. But when the construction note came due the department could not raise the necessary funds. The building was put up for sale and was purchased by the Woodmen of the World lodge. After this it became known as the WOW Hall.

After E.M. Tilley died on December 21, 1917, his home on Chesapeake Avenue was occupied by Quinton Clarence Davis Jr. and his family.

In 1919, Dean Preston constructed a large three-story building at 1 Chesapeake Avenue. Also in 1919, the Grand Theatre opened and the large vacant lot at the corner of Chesapeake Avenue and Ohio Street became the location of the Chesapeake Pharmacy.

A bill to incorporate the Town of South Norfolk was legislated and it became law on September 11, 1919. South Norfolk began to function as a town on September 19, 1919. Q.C. Davis Jr. was the first mayor and E.L. Harper was appointed president of the nine-member council. The town had assets of more than $4 million.

This picture of Dr. Nicholas George Wilson was taken ca.1905. Wilson was born September 13, 1871, at the family homestead on the Eastern Branch of the Elizabeth River in Norfolk County, Virginia. In his early years his grandmother tutored him and when he was about seven years of age he was enrolled in the Providence Public School about four miles away. After this he entered the Hemingway Private School in Norfolk, Virginia, from which he graduated in 1887.

Wilson graduated with the degree of doctor of medicine from the University of Maryland in 1895. Returning to Norfolk, he began the practice of medicine at the home of his Aunt Carrie Edwards on Liberty Street in South Norfolk, Virginia. *Photo courtesy of Kaye R. Herndon.*

This picture was taken June 9, 1909, at 13 Chesapeake Avenue in South Norfolk, the home of Dr. Nicholas G. Wilson. The occasion was the wedding day of John G. Wallace II and Mildred Wilson. *Top row, left to right:* Norfleet Etheridge, William M. Wallace, George T. Wallace II, Dr. Frank D. Wilson, Captain John G. Wallace, Dr. Nicholas G. Wilson and Charles B. Wilson. *Second row from the top:* Dr. Albert E. Wilson, Grace H. Wilson, Ruth W. Harrison, Georgie Halstead Etheridge and Verna Halstead Lamerdin. *Third row:* John G. Wallace II (groom), Mildred Wilson (bride), Beulah Halstead Wilson, Mrs. G.N. Halstead (Dr. G.N. Halstead had died in 1901) and W.L. Lamerdin Jr. *Fourth row:* Jennie Halstead Rountrey, Mildred Tyler Wilson, Mrs. William Wallace and either Margaret Wilson or Florence Rountrey. *Bottom row:* Nicholas G. Wilson Jr. This large house later became the J.R. Williams Funeral Home. *Photo courtesy of Kaye R. Herndon.*

The year was 1909 and this group gathered along the banks of the Elizabeth River. What was the occasion? No one knows for sure. Was it a baptism or did the crowd assemble to watch a fleet of ships? Whatever the reason, it must have been on Sunday afternoon because most of the people are well dressed. The railroad bridge can be seen in the right background. *Photos courtesy of Linwood L. Briggs Jr.*

One of the most important early developments was the processing of seabird droppings or guano. Farmers learned in the mid-nineteenth century that those droppings made a particularly effective fertilizer. In a busy horse and buggy era in Tarboro, North Carolina, this former country boy by the name of Frank Sheppard Royster opened his first fertilizer factory in 1885. In 1891, Royster sent his young protégé, Charles F. Burroughs Sr., to the area to start up production in a Berkley warehouse. Soon thereafter, the company built a large fertilizer plant in South Norfolk and operated under the name Columbia Guano Company. In 1898, Royster made Norfolk his permanent headquarters and on August 2, 1900, changed the firm's name to F.S. Royster Guano Company. In 1901, Royster built his home on the corner of Warren Crescent and Colonial Avenue in the Ghent section of Norfolk, Virginia. *Courtesy of Sargeant Memorial Room, Norfolk Public Library, Norfolk, Virginia.*

This early 1900s house was the home of D.W. Godwin, local contractor and builder. Its location was probably on Freeman Avenue in the section named Buell near Money Point. *Photo from the Hassell family collection.*

This class picture of Miss Huffman's third- and fourth-grade classes was taken in 1917. The name of the school is not known, however it is possible that it was one of the early wooden schools in Money Point. *Photo from the Hassell family collection.*

This small certificate from the Rosebud Missionary Society of the Virginia Conference of the Methodist Episcopal Church, South, was awarded to little Miss Mildred Virginia Simpkins on October 14, 1912. Miss Simpkins grew up and became Mrs. Francis Gay. She is now ninety-five years of age. *Courtesy of Mildred Gay.*

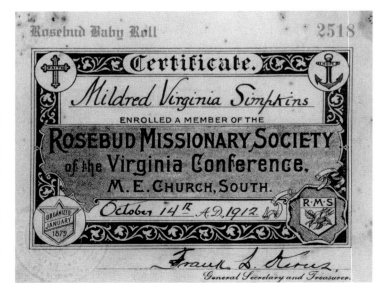

THE 1920s

By December 22, 1920, the population of South Norfolk was 7,691, and Mayor Davis prepared a petition for the town to become a city of the second class. On January 5, 1921, South Norfolk, pursuant to law, became a city of the second class, with Floyd L. Rowland as mayor; Q.C. Davis Jr., first city attorney; William T. Madrin, clerk; Paul M. Warden, city sergeant; S. Herman Dennis, treasurer; and E.H. Brown, commissioner of revenue.

A bond issue was floated in 1922 enabling the city to run sewer lines down the center of the principal streets. A two-lane concrete strip was paved down most of the streets. Those sewer lines, which were made of wood, are still buried beneath the roadway on Poindexter Street and are in use today. Work on Poindexter Street, which is scheduled to begin in August 2006, will replace the sewer and water lines and at the same time all electric wiring will be placed underground.

Also in 1922, a high school was built in the village of Portlock. The community at that time was still a part of Norfolk County. It became a town in 1948 and was annexed by the City of South Norfolk in 1951.

New construction continued throughout the 1920s and into the 1930s. The decade of the 1920s was a period of national prosperity. C.M. Jordan, W.P. Jordan and associates financed construction of the Norfolk-Portsmouth (Jordan) Bridge. Permission to build the bridge was received from the 69th Congress (Public Bill No. 272) on May 22, 1926. The construction cost was $1,125,000. The bridge opened for traffic on August 24, 1928.

In 1927, Irvin Truitt of Truitt-Smith Reality Corporation began development of a new residential section on part of the land that he had acquired from the heirs of William Nathaniel Portlock. This new development was given the name "Avalon."

By 1928, many new stores were beginning to appear on Poindexter and Liberty Streets, providing a larger shopping district. Also in 1928, I was born in the second story of the house located at 155 Commerce Street at the corner of Park Avenue. The first floor was home to the Young family. The house was demolished several years ago.

In the meantime, the schools on B Street became inadequate for the number of students and property for construction of a new high school was acquired on Holly Street. The new South Norfolk High School was built in 1929 at a cost of $140,430. The first students entered the school on February 3, 1930.

The seal of the City of South Norfolk. On September 19, 1919, the village of South Norfolk became a town, and on January 5, 1921, it became a city of the second class. *From the author's collection.*

This photograph of the South Norfolk High School junior class was taken December 8, 1921. Miss Lucille Scaff was the homeroom teacher. Approximately twenty years later she would become my math teacher. Miss Scaff never married; she lived about ninety-five years and spent her last years in a retirement home. *From the author's collection.*

W. Dean Preston became licensed to practice pharmacy in Virginia in 1912. In 1913, he purchased J.T. Lane's drug store on Liberty Street in South Norfolk and established Preston's Pharmacy. In 1938, he built a new store at the corner of Poindexter and B Streets. Preston had this large house built at the corner of D and Twenty-second Streets where he, his wife Molly and their son lived until moving to Kemp Lane. This ca. 1920 image is from a picture post card (the small boy in the front yard is probably Preston's son). This along with other picture post cards of South Norfolk scenes could be purchased at Preston's Pharmacy. *Photo courtesy of Stuart Smith.*

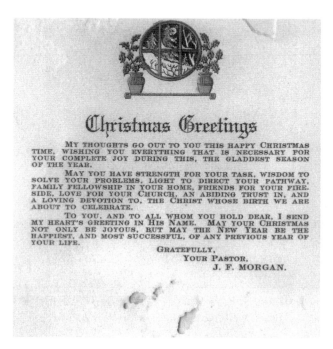

Pastor J.F. Morgan of the Rosemont Christian Church addressed this Christmas card to Mr. Chester Cahoon of Buell, Virginia. It was postmarked December 20, 1926. Buell is approximately one mile from the church near Money Point. *From the author's collection.*

The play *In Portlock Town* was presented February 4, 1927, by the Portlock High School Athletic Association. The cast was made up of fifteen members and the school chorus. Principal T.C. Anderson is the first man on the left in the second row. *Photo by Long Studios, Norfolk, Virginia. From the author's collection.*

Members of the Chesapeake Avenue Methodist Church held an oyster roast at Keeling Farm, Lynhaven Inlet, Virginia, on November 13, 1927. The photo was taken by Tidewater Photo Service of Norfolk, Virginia. *Photo courtesy of Anne Howell Maheu.*

C.M. Jordan and W.P. Jordan Jr., owners of the Jordan Brothers Lumber Company with offices at Park Avenue and Truxton Street in South Norfolk, Virginia, formed the Norfolk-Portsmouth Bridge Corporation in the 1920s and financed construction of the Norfolk-Portsmouth (Jordan) Bridge.

Messrs. Harrington, Howard and Ash, engineers from Kansas City, Missouri, designed the bridge, and E.R. Needles of the firm's New York office oversaw the construction. The contract was awarded to Atlantic Bridge Company, Inc., on June 25, 1927, and work started August 15, 1927. The cost to build the bridge was $1,125,000 and it opened for traffic on August 24, 1928.

The Jordan is a vertical-lift bridge, which has a section of roadway between two towers. The span crosses the Southern Branch of the Elizabeth River and links South Norfolk with Portsmouth. When this photograph was taken, C.M. Jordan was president of the corporation, E.R. Needles was civil engineer, the resident engineer was E.E. Paul and C. Hubard Massey was the road engineer. A large number of photographs were taken during construction and immediately after completion of the bridge. The title of this picture, which was taken February 2, 1928, is "Showing Progress." *From the author's collection.*

This photograph of the Norfolk-Portsmouth (Jordan) Bridge construction was taken March 1, 1928. It was number twenty in a large series of construction pictures. *From the author's collection.*

O. M. JORDAN, PRESIDENT

W. P. JORDAN, JR., SECY.-TREAS.

NORFOLK-PORTSMOUTH BRIDGE CORP.

L. D. TELEPHONE BERKLEY 796
OFFICE: PARK & TRUXTON STS.

SOUTH NORFOLK, VA.,
(MAIL ADDRESS: BOX 240, NORFOLK, VA.)

Sept. 21st, 1928.

Received of Norfolk-Portsmouth Corp. in good order the following: which are to be kept in the operator's house at all times:

One wash basin

One slop-jar

One well bucket

50' $\frac{1}{2}$" rope

I have personally checked up the above and placed them in the operator's house.

Operator,

[signature]

This inventory of the items to be kept in the bridge operator's house is dated September 21, 1928. Hopefully these items have been replaced by more modern and convenient ones. *From the author's collection.*

THE 1930s

A period of national prosperity followed World War I and new construction was at an all-time high. It was in October 1929 that strange things began to happen with the stock market. On October 23 there was a spectacular drop during the last hour of trading. The next day almost thirteen million shares changed hands. This day (October 24, 1929) became known in history as "Black Thursday." In spite of all this, a large number of new houses were built along Seaboard Avenue and other parts of South Norfolk.

On February 3, 1930, the new South Norfolk High School on Holly Street received its first students. In the spring of 1933, city attorney Q.C. Davis Jr. went to Washington, D.C., as chairman of a committee formed to acquire funds for construction of Lakeside Park. He was successful and work started in the summer. The job was done by hand, and many previously unemployed men were put to work. As a small boy I remember watching the men dig the lake using shovels and hauling the dirt away in wheelbarrows. Because the community had used the area for drainage, pumps were required to keep the water out while the men dug this large hole in the ground. Gravel walks were laid and a rustic bridge was built out of lumber donated by Carl Jordan of Jordan Lumber Company. Greenbrier Farms planted trees and shrubs. Plaques were placed in the ground at the base of each tree to commemorate those from South Norfolk who had died in World War I.

A familiar sight along the Southern Branch of the Elizabeth River was the steamboat *Emma Kay*. The *Emma Kay*, whose skipper was Captain Snow, brought produce from the farms of North Carolina to the Roanoke docks in Norfolk. It made several stops along the way and picked up a few passengers.

In 1937, the Portlock overpass, which stands near present-day Southgate Plaza shopping center, was constructed over the Virginian Railroad. Dirt for the overpass came from land owned by the Portlock family.

On September 2, 1939, Robert Rowland purchased the old Portlock farm and the farmhouse that had been built in 1854. The house was moved to Hamilton Street and now faces Mill Dam Creek. Mr. Rowland, along with Simeon Leary, developed the land and gave it the name "Portlock Terrace."

In 1939, the home of John Cuthrell, one of the most impressive homes in South Norfolk, was bought by Francis A. and Mildred Gay and was turned into a funeral home.

This picture of Jack Hassell was taken on Bainbridge Boulevard in front of the family car on January 17, 1930. The Portlock High School can be seen in the upper left background. It looks as if Santa Claus brought Jack a rifle of some kind—be careful, you'll shoot your eye out! *Photo from the Hassell family collection.*

These were two of the three school buildings on B Street. Construction of the one on the left was accomplished in 1902. The building on the right was ready to accept students in September 1910. The two buildings were connected by a hall. The building on the right was near Twenty-second Street and originally served as the high school. This photo was taken February 5, 1930. *Courtesy of Sargeant Memorial Room, Norfolk Public Library, Norfolk, Virginia.*

This photograph, which was taken on February 5, 1930, is of the first South Norfolk High School. Two days prior to this the first students entered the new high school on Holly Street. *Courtesy of Sargeant Memorial Room, Norfolk Public Library, Norfolk, Virginia.*

Facing page and above: These three photographs of Lakeside Park were taken in the spring of 1934 following the dedication of the park. *Photos courtesy of Anne Howell Maheu.*

The Norfolk terminal of the Texas Oil Company was opened in 1910 along the Southern Branch of the Elizabeth River in South Norfolk. The land on which the plant was built was filled. The plant initially processed gasoline but when it closed approximately ninety years later it was processing oil for lubrication. Many residents of South Norfolk and nearby communities spent their entire working years working for Texaco. This photograph of the terminal office was taken June 1, 1934. In later years a new brick office building was constructed. *Photo courtesy of Frankie Sweetwood.*

This was the Texaco parking garage, as it appeared December 3, 1935. *Photo courtesy of Frankie Sweetwood.*

Here we see the fair sex of the Norfolk terminal of the Texas Oil Company, Oretha Beale (left) and Eloise Gibney. The ladies posed for this picture, which appeared in the *Texaco Topics* magazine in September–October 1936. *Photo courtesy of Frankie Sweetwood.*

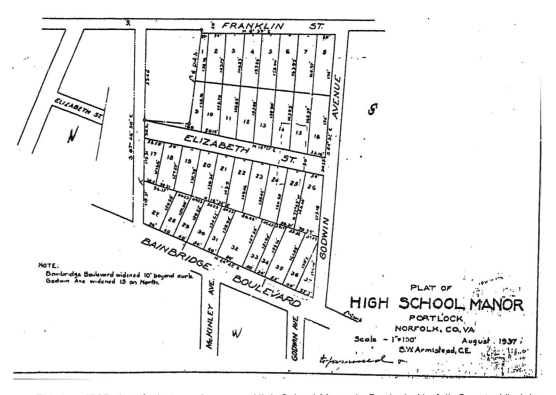

This is a 1937 plat of what was known as High School Manor in Portlock, Norfolk County, Virginia. Elizabeth Street no longer exists. *From the author's collection.*

This ca. 1930s photograph was taken in front of the Grand Theatre on Chesapeake Avenue. Each year in December, the theatre, in conjunction with the local Joy Fund, collected canned goods for the needy of South Norfolk. A special showing of cartoons and westerns took place on a Saturday mornings before Christmas. The price of admission was a can of food. The men in this picture are, from left to right, Ed Rease, owner of the Grand; Hunter Williams, from the Williams Funeral Home next to the theatre; A.B. (Bus) Howell, head of the South Norfolk Joy Fund; and George Leoffert, manager of the Grand Theatre. *From the author's collection.*

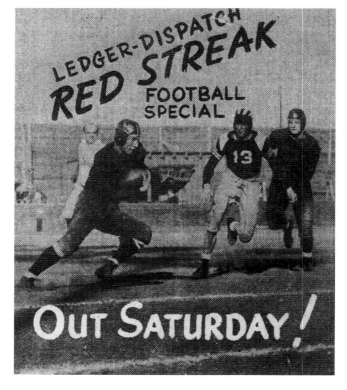

This football game between the Wilson High School Presidents and the South Norfolk High School Tigers was played on a Friday afternoon at Sewanee Stadium in Portsmouth. The man with the ball is Slade Phillips, a Wilson High School back. Number 13 is South Norfolk High School's Otho (Squinchy) Horton. The other player is unidentified. Wilson won the game by a score of 39–0. Back in those days South Norfolk just could not beat Wilson High School. Ca. 1939. *From the author's collection.*

This picture of the official South Norfolk family was taken in front of the newly remodeled municipal building on Liberty Street after its completion in 1938. They are, from left to right, W.M. Townsend, city treasurer; Claude W. Davis, city councilman; H.P. Lane, commissioner of revenue; W.T. Madren, clerk of the common council; J. James Davis Sr., mayor; unknown; C.H. Hughes, director of public works; E.E. Henley, city councilman; C.F. Abbott, city councilman; C.F. Whitley, city attorney; A.B. Howell, city councilman; Herman White, trial justice; and unknown. *Photo courtesy of J. James Davis Jr.*

This 1930s picture is of Sam Creef's Texaco service station at the corner of Poindexter and B Streets. The grocery store of his brother Seldon Creef can be seen in the right background facing B Street. *From the author's collection.*

The Phelps brothers—left to right, Earl, Willie and Norman—made up the Virginia Rounders. At one time they were known as Norman Phelps and the Virginia Rounders. They performed on the rodeo circuit for a while and then, in 1936, headed for Hollywood, appearing in several westerns as singing cowboys. In 1938, they decided to return to Virginia where they continued to play country western music. The Phelps brothers grew up on Hull Street in South Norfolk. *From the author's collection.*

These were the gatemen of the Norfolk terminal of the Texas Oil Company. This photograph, which was taken in 1939, appeared in the September–October issue of *Texaco Topics*, the company magazine. The men are, from left to right, F.W. Ward, F.A. Jones and W.J. Daily. *Photo courtesy of Frankie Sweetwood.*

This Christmas tree print was first used in 1924. At the beginning of December each child in the Sunday school class received a copy. The stick-on candles indicate the number of Sundays attended during the month. I received my copy from the South Norfolk Christian Church in the early 1930s. *From the author's collection.*

Dave Gillard's Texaco station was located at 2014 Bainbridge Boulevard in the early 1930s. At that time the area was known as Jones's Switch. A few years later it was demolished and Squatty Ferrell built his restaurant at that location. The building later became Grace's Beauty Salon and at this time an antiques dealer is doing business there. *Drawing by Richard Spratley.*

Pictured here at the Norfolk terminal of the Texas Oil Company are trucks from Bass Bonded Trucks, Inc., in Tarboro, North Carolina. *Photo courtesy of Frankie Sweetwood.*

This photograph shows the *Pawtucket* tied up at the docks of the Texas Company along the Southern Branch of the Elizabeth River in South Norfolk. *Photo courtesy of Frankie Sweetwood.*

This is John Greenough, catcher for the South Norfolk High School Tigers. This picture was taken on the Twentieth Street side of the South Norfolk Grammar School, ca. 1939. The house in the background was covered with dark green wooden shingles. It was the only house in that block of Twentieth Street. At one time it was the home of Billy Black and his family. *From the author's collection.*

THE 1940s

By 1940, the country had weathered the Great Depression and in December 1941, the United States was forced to enter World War II. The war touched the lives of every family in one way or another. Those in a certain age bracket answered our country's call, and all remember the draft board on A Street in South Norfolk.

With the outset of the war and the many shortages that accompanied it, rationing became a way of life. In May 1942, the Office of Price Administration (OPA) opened local board, number 48-65-4, at 701 Saint James Street, where rationing books were issued to the families of South Norfolk. Before the war ended in 1945, gasoline, tires, fuel oil, shoes, meats, sugar and most other food items were rationed. When the war ended, many of those who had not finished high school used the GI Bill and returned to the classroom. Most high school graduates took advantage of the opportunity afforded by the GI Bill and enrolled in college.

In 1947, the newly formed Junior Chamber of Commerce petitioned the city to change the form of government from the mayor council to the city manager form. A referendum was held on April 1, 1947, and the vote was 669 for and 501 against. The new form of government went into effect on September 1, 1947.

On March 18, 1948, the village of Portlock was chartered as a town. The township was short lived because, in October 1949, South Norfolk won its bid for annexation of the Town of Portlock. At that time, the court suggested July 1, 1950, as the effective date of the decree.

During the month of December each year several local businesses prepared and delivered food baskets to the needy families of the community. This photograph was taken in December 1940. The man on the left is A.B. (Bus) Howell. *Photo courtesy of Frankie Sweetwood.*

All the employees of the Texas Oil Company looked forward to the annual picnic. In 1941, it was held on September 27. The man on the left end is Herbert Curtis, the fourth man from the left is A.B. (Bus) Howell and the man on his left is Marty Malaney. *Photo courtesy of Frankie Sweetwood.*

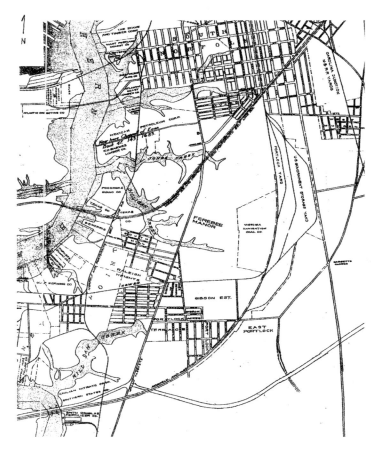

This map of South Norfolk and Portlock and surrounding areas was drawn after 1937, possibly ca.1940. The Avalon section of South Norfolk, which was developed in 1937, can be seen near the top center. Between Scuffletown and Jones Creeks near Barnes Road was the location of the third chapel of the Elizabeth River Parish and on the map is a notation that states "Near here Chapell of Ease – Book 4F. Page 143 1683." From time to time someone will try to prove that the chapel was built somewhere other than South Norfolk, but the proof can be found in the records at the office of the clerk of the Chesapeake Circuit Court. A close look at this map will also reveal many of the industrial plants along the Southern Branch of the Elizabeth River. *From the author's collection.*

Snow has blanketed the small city of South Norfolk. This ca. 1940 picture of Hardy Forbes (on the right) and his unidentified friend was taken on the grammar school yard on B Street near Twenty-second Street. The WOW Hall on Twenty-second Street is in the background. At the right side of the building is an alley that connects Twenty-second Street to the 1400 block of Poindexter Street. This is not a good day to ride a bicycle because it's possible that you could slip and land on your backside. *Photo courtesy of Hardy Forbes.*

Here is South Norfolk High School on June 4, 1940. A close inspection will reveal that all the windows were open—hot weather had arrived. There were no air-conditioned schools in 1940. As a matter of fact, there were no air-conditioned homes. *Courtesy of Sargeant Memorial Room, Norfolk Public Library, Norfolk, Virginia.*

In early 1942, the Office of Price Administration (OPA) was formed and everyone received War Ration Books. Local board 48-65-4 was located at 701 Saint James Street in South Norfolk. This is the cover of one of my ration books. When entering the military your books had to be turned in to the local rationing board. *From the author's collection.*

Here is South Norfolk's municipal building, as it appeared ca. 1943. The building was originally constructed on Liberty Street in the early 1930s and remodeled in 1938. This main entrance was on the side near the approach to the overpass. The two large trees were decorated with colored lights each year during the Christmas season. *Courtesy of Sargeant Memorial Room, Norfolk Public Library, Norfolk, Virginia.*

Pictured here is a part of Lane's Row in 1943. The business visible on the left is the Goodrich Tire Store. They also sold bicycles. I bought my one and only bicycle there in the early 1940s. Would you believe a new Schwinn bike sold for $24.95? Next to the tire store was McHorney's restaurant. His first customers each day were the newspaper carriers. We all had a Dixie cup of ice cream for breakfast. Around 1900 this was the location of Harper's Hardware. Next to McHorney's was Claude Baker's hardware store. In the latter 1800s this was the location of J.T. Lane's drug store. In 1913, Dean Preston bought Lane's store and this was the first location of Preston's Pharmacy. *From the author's collection.*

During World War II, most industrial plants become involved by producing equipment essential to the war effort. Those that met or surpassed their quotas were awarded the Army and Navy E (for efficiency) flag.

Pictured here and in the next five photographs are members of the U.S. Army, Navy and Coast Guard: South Norfolk Mayor J. James Davis; Reverend O.D. Poythress, pastor of the South Norfolk Christian Church; and officials of the J.G. Wilson Corporation. They are assembled at the corporation office building for this very important occasion. *Photo courtesy of J. James Davis Jr.*

Reverend O.D. Poythress is the fourth man from the left and Mayor Davis is seated behind the podium. The man holding the microphone is the representative from the U.S. Army. *Photo courtesy of J. James Davis Jr.*

Here we see Mayor Davis addressing the guests and employees of the J.G. Wilson Corporation. *Photo courtesy of J. James Davis Jr.*

In this picture two officials of the J.G. Wilson Corporation are holding the flag. This is what it is all about. The employees have worked hard and now their efforts are being recognized by the presentation of this symbol of honor. *Photo courtesy of J. James Davis Jr.*

In this distant shot we see the corporation officials and a part of the audience holding the flag. Two army men can be seen near the flagpole. It is their job to receive the flag and run it up the pole where it will join the American and one other flag. *Photo courtesy of J. James Davis Jr.*

In this image we see the two soldiers raising the new E flag. As can be seen by the sign on the front of the building, the J.G. Wilson Corporation was established in 1876. It became a part of the South Norfolk industrial community in 1903. The plant employed residents of South Norfolk and nearby communities for almost one hundred years. *Photo courtesy of J. James Davis Jr.*

John Burfoot's Esso station was located at the corner of Poindexter and Liberty Streets in August 1944. The small building behind it at 1425 Poindexter Street is the office of Snell Brothers' taxi. It later served as the insurance office of Dick Arnold. *From the author's collection.*

This picture of Presley Curling was taken in August 1945. Curling passed away suddenly on December 11, 2005. He served in the First Calvary Division and was in the Asiatic-Pacific Theater during World War II. He was a recipient of the Purple Heart and the Bronze Star. *Photo and information courtesy of his daughter Susan Curling Watts.*

William M. Tuck was governor of the Commonwealth of Virginia from January 1946 to January 17, 1950. He is the man on the left seen here shaking hands with South Norfolk Mayor J. James Davis. *Photo courtesy of J. James Davis Jr.*

These four men of political importance are standing next to the municipal building on Liberty Street in South Norfolk. They are, from left to right, South Norfolk director of public works, Charley Hughes; South Norfolk mayor, J. James Davis; governor of Virginia, William Munford Tuck; and the first mayor of the Town of South Norfolk, Q.C. Davis Jr. This picture was taken ca. 1948. *Photo courtesy of J. James Davis Jr.*

The South Norfolk Community Football League was organized in 1944. The first year there were four teams: the Junior Chamber of Commerce (Jaycees), coached by James Benton and Billy Black; the Knights of Pythias, coached by Jim Burton; the American Legion, coached by Mike Smith; and the Odd Fellows, coached by David Pierce. The members of this later team, possibly 1945, are, from left to right, (front row) Signal Lee, Nelson Odom, Eugene Goodrich, unknown and Harry Farmer; (middle row) William Horton, Jerome Greenough, Calvin Sykes, Jesse Hardison and Jimmie Marshall; (back row) Billy Black (coach), Roger Jordan, Norman Bunting, James Maples, Lenville Wilson, Warren Morse, Sidney Johnson and David Pierce (coach). *Photo courtesy of Anne Howell Maheu.*

Here is another South Norfolk Community Football team. Unfortunately it is not possible to name all the members seen here. The identifiable members are, from left to right, (front row) Henry Early, unknown, unknown, Ray Dillon and Phil Dowdy; (middle row) unknown, Allen Russ, Bobby Long, unknown and unknown; (back row) Raymond Mott, Bruce (Geese) Pillow, Edward Harris, Bernard (Bunky) Womack, Gordon Dillon and unknown (coach). *Photo courtesy of Anne Howell Maheu.*

In the 1940s Duncan's confectionery store sponsored a softball team by the name of Dunk's Punks. The team consisted mostly of young men from South Norfolk High School. This photograph is of a classmate of mine, Sidney Johnson. Sid was well known throughout the entire state for his fastball—and I mean fast—you could hardly see it! *Photo courtesy of Anne Howell Maheu.*

Nelson Bondurant, who was originally from Portlock, was the catcher for Dunk's Punks. He later served as clerk of the South Norfolk court. *Photo courtesy of Anne Howell Maheu.*

Jimmie Clark was another member of Dunk's team. I am not sure what position he played. *Photo courtesy of Anne Howell Maheu.*

Bill Ervin, another member of the team, appears to be waiting his turn at bat. He is seen here displaying his trophy. From his position in the photo I would guess he received it for his batting successes. *Photo courtesy of Anne Howell Maheu.*

Upon returning home from the military after World War II, Bennie White opened this Sinclair service station on Bainbridge Boulevard near Admiral Roads. The vehicle seen on the right side of the station was an old funeral home hearse, which was used to provide road service. The house to the left of the station was the home of Grover White. *Photo courtesy of Bennie White Jr.*

Most early service stations furnished a gathering place for men of the nearby neighborhood. White's was no exception. These men inside White's station are, from left to right, Cecil (Snookie) White, Bennie White Sr., Jesse Phelps, Arthur Lee (Mugs) Martin, another friend and Jiggs the dog. *Photo courtesy of Bennie White Jr.*

On Christmas Eve 1947, it began to snow about midday and continued through Christmas Day. This created a rather large accumulation of the fluffy white stuff, requiring a considerable amount of shoveling. This large pile of snow in front of White's Sinclair station provided a mountain for young Bennie White Jr. to climb. *Photo courtesy of Bennie White Jr.*

This ca. 1948 photograph of Sharon Curling was taken in front of the family home at 608 B Street in South Norfolk. This picture furnishes a nice view of the B Street neighborhood as it was in 1948. I lived at 608 B Street from about 1930 until April 1932. *Photo courtesy of Susan Curling Watts.*

This cute young lady is Diane Walls. The picture was taken in the 1940s on Twentieth Street. The large building on the right is part of the South Norfolk Grammar School on B Street. In the distance and to the left can be seen the bowling alley and the fire station on Liberty Street. *From the author's collection.*

These men were members of the Woodmen of the World Lodge. Their usual meeting place was the WOW Hall on Twenty-second Street in South Norfolk. However, this ca. 1942 presentation was made in the South Norfolk Christian Church. The men are, from left to right, unknown, Henry Rawls, Hugh Rawls, unknown and Reverend O.D. Poythress, pastor of the church. *Photo by H.A. Stewart Jr. and courtesy of Lou Trzinski.*

In 1949, Duval Flora ran for treasurer of the City of South Norfolk. Mr. Claude McPherson painted this sign, which was mounted on Michael Flora's tricycle. Michael was about three months short of being four years old at that time; however, he wasn't too young to campaign for his dad. On November 8, 1949, Duval Flora became treasurer of South Norfolk and after the merger with Norfolk County he became the first treasurer of the City of Chesapeake. Flora retired in 1989 with forty years' service as treasurer of South Norfolk and Chesapeake. What about Michael? He turned sixty years old February 12, 2006, and is a supervisor with the state department of taxation. *Photo courtesy of N. Duval and Michael Flora.*

It was 1:30 p.m. on November 11, 1949, when this Armistice Day parade got underway. The Boy Scouts of America were well represented. When this picture was taken the troop was passing the Portlock Elementary School. One corner of the high school building can be seen in the upper right corner; also there is a new 1949 Ford parked in the distance at the foot of the fire escape. *From the author's collection.*

THE 1950s

Before the annexation, South Norfolk covered an area approximately five miles by seven miles. With the annexation, the area increased by 225 percent, and the population reached 20,896. With this increase, the requirement to become a city of the first class was met, and shortly thereafter South Norfolk became a first-class city.

Continued increase in school enrollment called for other schools to be built. Early in 1950, the City of South Norfolk purchased twenty-six acres at the foot of Rodgers Street. It was there that the first Oscar Frommel Smith High School was built at a cost of about $1 million. Students occupied the school in September 1954. Forty years later, this became a middle school and a new Oscar Frommel Smith High School opened on Great Bridge Boulevard.

In February 1953, South Norfolk received its own corporation court, and Q.C. Davis Jr. became the first judge. In the latter part of 1953, construction of a new corporation court building was begun between the municipal building and the combination fire and police building.

In 1957, Linwood L. Briggs Jr. became mayor and served until September 1961. At that time Charles Richardson succeeded Briggs and became the last mayor of the City of South Norfolk.

This was our Christmas tree at 708 Stewart Street in 1950. It was Emma's and my second Christmas as man and wife. That was the year that I got my one and only Lionel train. It can be seen running beneath the tree. *From the author's collection.*

This photograph was taken from the 1200 block of Rodgers Street in June 1958. The intersection of Rodgers and Ohio Streets can be seen as well as part of the 1100 block of Rodgers Street. *From the author's collection.*

This is an aerial view of the J.G. Wilson plant in South Norfolk near the Jordan Bridge. The J.G. Wilson Corporation became an important part of the industrial area of South Norfolk in 1903 and remained in business for almost one hundred years. This photograph was taken ca. 1954. *From the author's collection.*

This small barbershop was located near the intersection of Portlock Road and Bainbridge Boulevard in the 1950s. There is a sign (which cannot be seen) in the window stating that haircuts were seventy-five cents. *From the author's collection.*

In November 1954, Dick Harrell, Allen Harris and Al Wagner Jr. opened Southern Office Supply Company in this old converted house at 802 Liberty Street. Sam and Kelly Dozier owned the building. Originally the structure had been a two-story house. Like many homeowners during the Great Depression, the owner of this house converted a part of the first floor into a store and lived in the rest of the house. When this picture was taken the building had settled and the floors were far from being level. *Photo courtesy of Dick Harrell.*

On February 19, 1955, employees of the Norfolk terminal of the Texas Oil Company were enjoying an oyster roast on property owned by the company. *Photo courtesy of Frankie Sweetwood.*

In spite of the cold weather on February 19, 1955, employees of the Texas Oil Company bundled up and enjoyed several bushels of roasted oysters. *Photo courtesy of Frankie Sweetwood.*

On May 6, 1955, the five-pointers from the Portlock elementary school were making preparations for their annual parade. This photograph was taken in the vicinity of where the South Norfolk Community Center is today. *Photo courtesy of Elizabeth Johnson.*

This photograph was also taken on May 6, 1955. Most of the schoolchildren are holding their stars in preparation for the upcoming five-pointer parade. The houses in the background are on Bainbridge Boulevard. The back of the post office on Godwin Avenue can be seen in the upper left part of the picture. *Photo courtesy of Elizabeth Johnson.*

The formal dedication of the Captain Frederic E. Consolvo Jr. Armory took place on May 12, 1956. The daylong activities began at 11:00 a.m. with a parade of National Guardsmen. A luncheon for more than one thousand guests followed the dedication. An open house was held in the afternoon and early evening and the night included a formal military ball. This photo, which was taken from above the activities, shows several couples enjoying themselves on the dance floor. It also shows that the armory was laid out and marked off for playing basketball. *Photo courtesy of Mrs. Clarence Forehand.*

This is another view of the interior of the armory as it was on May 12, 1956. Fifty years have now passed since the dedication and other activities of that proud moment in the history of the City of South Norfolk. The unoccupied building still stands, but has been allowed to deteriorate to the point where it will probably be demolished in the near future. *Photo courtesy of Mrs. Clarence Forehand.*

This June 1958 tree planting in Lakeside Park was attended by Mayor Linwood L. Briggs Jr., City Manager Phil Davis, Deputy Fire Chief W.H. (Wink) Evans and one other member of the South Norfolk Fire Department. *Photo courtesy of Linwood L. Briggs Jr.*

On May 27, 1957, Mrs. Princess Gibson's third grade class posed for this picture. The fifth student from the front in the first row on the left (next to the window) is Raymond T. Jones. His seat was next to the window where he could see all the cars that went into the Esso station and keep a tally of the amount of gas sold. In other words, he wasn't paying much attention to what went on in class. Some years later a school counselor advised him to learn a trade because he was not college material. Raymond did in fact attend college where he received undergraduate, master's and doctorate degrees. To add to all this he spent twenty-two years in the Chesapeake school system before becoming vice-president of public radio services at station WHRO in Norfolk, Virginia. *From the author's collection.*

This was the intersection of Poindexter and Liberty Streets in March 1957. *From the author's collection.*

UNITED STATES JUNIOR CHAMBER OF COMMERCE

Spark Plug

CERTIFICATE OF ACCOMPLISHMENT

This is to certify that

N. Hodges
of the
South Norfolk

Junior Chamber of Commerce

has fulfilled the requirements of this award by his continuous and active participation in the activities of his organization.

Dated this **23rd** day of **January** 19**57**

H. L. Chitim
LOCAL PRESIDENT

Nathan R. Heatwole
STATE PRESIDENT

Kenneth D. Ulis
NATIONAL LEADERSHIP DEVELOPMENT CHAIRMAN

This certificate of accomplishment was awarded by the United States Chamber of Commerce to Norman Hodges Jr. of the South Norfolk Junior Chamber of Commerce on January 23, 1957. *Courtesy of Norman Hodges III.*

In this photograph, Norman Hodges Jr. is holding a proposed license plate to commemorate the 350th anniversary of the landing at Jamestown. The Virginia Department of Motor Vehicles turned it down. The reason given was that it might distract other drivers and cause accidents. Have you noticed Virginia license plates recently? *Photo courtesy of Norman Hodges III.*

A few years before the merger of the City of South Norfolk with Norfolk County, urban renewal was a hot topic. Many photographs were taken and plans were made to abolish slums and build new housing for those who lost their homes in the process. This was one of those photographs. *Courtesy of Sargeant Memorial Room, Norfolk Public Library, Norfolk, Virginia.*

Here we see several children at play in one of the playground areas in South Norfolk. *Courtesy of Sargeant Memorial Room, Norfolk Public Library, Norfolk, Virginia.*

Peebles and Meacom Service Center was located at 130 East Liberty Street in 1954. This place of business was very near the boundary line between South Norfolk and Berkley. *From the author's collection.*

William J. (Bill) Berry operated his painting contractor business out of his home at 1327 Twentieth Street in South Norfolk. In this picture Edward Berry, Bill's brother, is the first man on the left and William J. (Bill) Berry is third from the left end. The Berry brothers were neighbors of mine in the 1100 block of Seaboard Avenue. *From the author's collection.*

The first Oscar Frommel Smith High School opened on Rodgers Street in South Norfolk in September 1954. This photograph shows the entrance to the new stadium. *Courtesy of Sargeant Memorial Room, Norfolk Public Library, Norfolk, Virginia.*

This is the new Oscar Frommel Smith High School in South Norfolk after its completion in 1954. The first class entered in September 1954. *From the author's collection.*

DEDICATION PROGRAM
OSCAR FROMMEL SMITH HIGH SCHOOL
South Norfolk, Virginia — May 18, 1955, 8:00 p.m.
School Auditorium

Invocation_____Rev. Frank Hughes
South Norfolk Baptist Church

Welcome_____Miss Aurelia Leigh

Introduction of Honor Guests_____Mr. William J. Story, Jr.
Superintendent of Schools

Tribute to Mr. Oscar Frommel Smith_____Mr. Ben Willis

Musical Selections:
    Land of Hope and Glory_____*Elgar*
    They Call It America_____*Grant*
    Oscar Frommel Smith High School Chorus_____Miss Anne Dove
Director

Presentation of Keys to Building:
    Mr. A. Ray Pentecost, Architect, to Mr. W. Roy Britton
    Mr. Britton, School Board Chairman, presents keys to Miss Leigh

Tribute to the Faculty_____Miss Patricia Nicholas
President, S.C.A.

Presentation of United States Flag:
    Mrs. David C. George_____Regent Borough of Norfolk
Daughters of American Revolution
    Mrs. W. Roy Britton_____Vice-Regent Borough of Norfolk
Daughters of American Revolution
    Mrs. P▮▮▮▮-Harris_____Borough of Norfolk
Daughters of American Revolution
Oath of Allegiance_____Audience Standing

Presentation of State Flag:
    Mrs. Laura Bozeman_____M.E.C. Willie Lee Temple #11
Pythian Sisters

Presentation of Bible:
    Mrs. Nellie Eason_____Councilor, Good Will Council #5
Daughters of America

Acceptance of Gifts_____Miss Leigh

Introduction of Speaker_____Mr. Story

Speech_____Hon. J. Lindsey Almond
Attorney-General of Virginia

Prayer of Dedication_____Phillip Davis
President-Elect, S.C.A.

This is a program from the dedication of the first Oscar Frommel Smith High School, which was held on May 18, 1955. *From the author's collection.*

This picture was taken in the school auditorium during the dedication of the Oscar Frommel Smith High School in South Norfolk, Virginia, on May 18, 1955, at 8:00 p.m. *Courtesy of Sargeant Memorial Room, Norfolk Public Library, Norfolk, Virginia.*

Roy Britton, chairman of the South Norfolk School Board, and William J. Story, superintendent of schools, are seen here pointing out the site for the new high school building that opened in September 1954. This picture was taken in 1953. The land at the foot of Rodgers Street was purchased from the Commonwealth of Virginia. *From the author's collection.*

This picture, which was taken from the second floor of the South Norfolk municipal building in 1954, shows a busy part of what was known as downtown South Norfolk. The entrance to the overpass and the stores in Lane's Row can be seen on the left. Monroe's drug store is slightly right of center. The bus in the picture is heading north along Liberty Street. There are several signs and a birdbath on the lawn straight ahead from the municipal building. The signs were usually military recruiting posters. *Courtesy of Sargeant Memorial Room, Norfolk Public Library, Norfolk, Virginia.*

This photograph was taken from the steps of the South Norfolk municipal building on a rainy afternoon in 1954. The curve in the center of the picture is the entrance to the South Norfolk overpass. The Ben Franklin store in the distant center is on Poindexter Street. Keatley's Motors and Lane's Row are on the left. The Esso station across the street is at the corner of Poindexter and Liberty Streets. The Pure Oil station is facing Liberty Street and is at the corner of Twenty-second Street. The Merchant and Planters Bank is at the corner of Liberty and Twenty-second Streets. When this picture was taken the street crossing the overpass was considered to be a part of Poindexter Street. With all the changes that have taken place, today it is considered to be part of Twenty-second Street. *Courtesy of Sargeant Memorial Room, Norfolk Public Library, Norfolk, Virginia.*

Every book that I have written about South Norfolk always has one or more pictures of Lakeside Park. It is such a beautiful park and it is very photogenic. Please allow me to include one more scene of the lake and the bridge crossing it. This photograph was taken more than fifty-one years ago, on September 9, 1954. *Courtesy of Sargeant Memorial Room, Norfolk Public library, Norfolk, Virginia.*

As can be seen by the sign in front of the building, this is the rental office for the Admiral's Road Apartments that were built during World War II to help alleviate the shortage of housing. Prior to the war this area was a part of Johnson's woods, and Bainbridge Boulevard came to an end at Poindexter Street. However, on the other side of the woods were a few houses on what was called Bainbridge Extended. When the war came the woods were cleared and four hundred apartments were constructed on that land. *Courtesy of Sargeant Memorial Room, Norfolk Public Library, Norfolk, Virginia.*

In 1902, Joseph Herbert Norton, who lived on Chesapeake Avenue, opened the Shirtwaist Factory in this building at the corner of Rodgers and Poindexter Streets. The Norfolk County Court chartered the factory in July. On July 30, 1902, the *Virginian-Pilot* newspaper announced that the factory was ready to start operation in ten days and would employ about one hundred people. Sometime later, Norton moved the factory to Thirteenth and Liberty Streets; it was then that a Mr. Hofner, who owned the building, turned it into apartments. Kline Chevrolet eventually bought the property and when this picture was taken in November 1951, the Southside Wrecking Company was demolishing the structure. The houses behind the building are on Rodgers Street. At least one of these homes was built in 1898. The Dairy Lane can be seen near the right end of the Hofner building. *Courtesy of Sargeant Memorial Room, Norfolk Public Library, Norfolk, Virginia.*

Let the work begin. The tanker *Wyoming* that is docked at the Norfolk terminal of the Texas Oil Company along the Southern Branch of the Elizabeth River stands ready to load all these barrels of oil on board, ca. 1952. *Photo courtesy of Frankie Sweetwood.*

The firm of A.S. Lee & Sons Company, Inc., manufacturers of agricultural lime and fertilizer, had its factory on Barnes Road along the Southern Branch of the Elizabeth River. In December 1933, Walter B. Mann and his associates acquired the business. At that time it became the Reliance Fertilizer and Lime Corporation. After Mann's death in March 1947, James Justin Joyce became president and Marguerite Joyce Mann of South Norfolk became vice-president. This photograph of Reliance Fertilizer and Lime Corporation was taken ca.1950s. *Photo courtesy of Hunter Joyce Burt.*

These men were members of the Jordan Bridge Commission. Those standing are, left to right, Paul Smith, William Warren, Herbert Hall, J. James Davis Sr., Nathan Sykes Jr. and Frank Wood. Seated, left to right, are William (Doc) Monroe and Webster Townsend. Ca. 1950s. *Photo courtesy of J. James Davis Jr.*

The Belt Line Railroad began serving as a link for the major railroads in the Norfolk-Portsmouth area in 1898. It operated with coal-burning steam locomotives from that time until 1955. Number 101, the first diesel, went into service on Christmas Day. *Photo courtesy of Richard Spratley.*

The original Norfolk and Portsmouth Belt Line Railroad Bridge was built in 1897–98. At that time sailing vessels were propelled by steam and drew no more than 17 feet of water. They rarely exceeded 240 feet in length and 45 feet in width. As time went on tankers measuring 542 feet in length and 75 feet in width and drawing 35 feet of water found it a dangerous process getting through the narrow swing span. Special pilots and additional tugs had to be used to maneuver the larger ships through the span. In 1957, a contract in the amount of $1,724,644.67 was awarded to the American Bridge Division of U.S. Steel Corporation for erection of the superstructure of the new bridge. This photograph shows early construction of the new Belt Line Bridge. *Photo courtesy of Richard Spratley.*

Here is a 1957 overhead view of a new diesel locomotive crossing the old swing bridge. *Photo courtesy of Richard Spratley.*

A previous contract in the amount of $388,000 was awarded to the Lang Construction Company of Hampton for bridge approaches and nine foundation piers. This photograph is of cofferdam pier number 3, looking east. A cofferdam is a temporary watertight enclosure for construction or repairs in waterlogged soil or under water. This picture was taken February 1,1956. *Photo courtesy of Richard Spratley.*

This view is looking northwest across cofferdam pier number 5, showing seal concrete being placed. This photograph was taken June 20, 1957. *Photo courtesy of Richard Spratley.*

This January 9, 1958 photograph was taken from the existing swing bridge and is directed southwest showing a portion of falsework span number 4, and also girder spans 1, 2, and 3. *Photo courtesy of Richard Spratley.*

The nine-hundred-ton center span of the new Norfolk and Portsmouth Belt Line Railroad Bridge was installed on June 30, 1958, marking completion of the bridge. The center span of the new bridge lined up with that of the Jordan Bridge, thus eliminating the dogleg course between the two bridges and improving navigation on the Southern Branch of the Elizabeth River. *Photo courtesy of Richard Spratley.*

The old Belt Line Railroad swing bridge can be seen near the bottom center of this aerial photograph. The Jordan is the vertical-lift bridge in the center and the ghost fleet can be seen to its right. *Photo courtesy of Richard Spratley.*

THE 1960s

Before the end of 1961, meetings were being held between Norfolk County politicians and the five-member South Norfolk city council. At these meetings, a merger was discussed. Beginning in January 1962, merger meetings were held with citizens from both Norfolk County and South Norfolk. Tuesday, February 13, 1962, was set as the date for the merger referendum. The consolidation was approved by a vote of 6,648 to 3,432. The next step was to be granted a charter by the General Assembly of Virginia.

After receiving approval from the General Assembly, it was decided that a name for the new city would be chosen in a later referendum. A total of twelve names appeared on the ballot. The name Chesapeake received 3,130 votes and the next highest was Great Bridge with 1,883. Chesapeake was the winner. With all of this political maneuvering accomplished, the City of Chesapeake came into being on January 1, 1963.

The Norfolk terminal of the Texas Oil Company can be seen at the top left of this aerial photograph. The large plant in the upper right is Cargill Incorporated. This operation is now Perdue Farms and is located at 505 Barnes Road. *Photo courtesy of Frankie Sweetwood.*

In this image we see a Texaco tanker being assisted by tugboats. The Norfolk terminal is near the right center of the photograph. *Photo courtesy of Frankie Sweetwood.*

This ca. 1960 picture shows Greenough & Co. Hardware and Building Supplies in the 1700 block of Park Avenue in South Norfolk. The fire, which destroyed the business, occurred on what was probably the coldest night of the year. The street is covered with ice from the fire hoses. *From the author's collection.*

This is the triple-decker overpass, as it appeared ca. 1960. Bainbridge Boulevard is the straight road passing under the bridge. The next level is the railroad bridge and the top of the overpass is Military Highway. *From the author's collection.*

The flooding conditions seen here at the Texaco plant in Portlock were as a result of the Ash Wednesday storm on March 7, 1962. The weather was really strange. Most areas received a light dusting of snow as well as high tides. *Photo courtesy of Frankie Sweetwood.*

In 1962, Dick Harrell had this new building erected and moved Southern Office Supply from Liberty Street to Bainbridge Boulevard. *Photo courtesy of Dick Harrell.*

This photo of Creekmore Hardware at 1303 Bainbridge Boulevard and the corner of Jefferson Street was taken in June 1962. If you can't find what you need at Creekmore's, it's a safe bet that you won't find it anywhere else. *Photo courtesy of Jimmy and Mike Creekmore.*

D.D. Jones Transfer & Warehouse Co., Inc., can be seen here in this ca. 1965 photograph at what is now 630 Twenty-second Street. In my youth this was a part of Poindexter Street. *From the author's collection.*

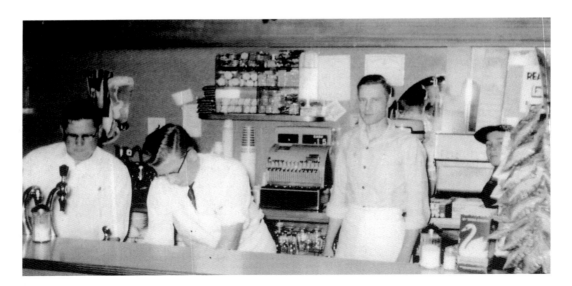

In 1919, R.C. Gilliam opened Chesapeake Pharmacy at the corner of Chesapeake Avenue and Ohio Street. Around 1936, Mr. Butt, who owned the pharmacy at the corner of Poindexter and Liberty Streets, bought the business from Gilliam and renamed it Butt Pharmacy No. 2. The following year he sold the store on Poindexter Street to William Monroe. By 1939, Butt had sold the store on Chesapeake Avenue to Albert Tatum who changed the name to Tatum's Pharmacy. In early 1949, Tatum sold the pharmacy to Dick Scharff who changed the name back to Chesapeake Pharmacy and that brings us to where we are in this photograph. This picture of the soda fountain crew was taken in 1965. They are, from left to right, Bud Dillon, Bill Elliott, Louis Chappell and an unknown young man standing behind the rack of potato chips. These grown men were all part-time help. Bill Elliott was employed full time at the Ford plant and worked at the pharmacy in the evenings for a period of five years. *Photo courtesy of Bill Elliott.*

This bank was built on land formerly occupied by Lane's Row on Liberty Street in South Norfolk. It was originally the Bank of South Norfolk at the corner of Liberty and Twenty-second Streets and later it became Merchants and Planters Bank. After that the name changed many times and today it is the Bank of America. This picture was taken in March 1967. *From the author's collection.*

This aerial view of the South Norfolk overpass and surrounding businesses was taken in 1967. We see here the intersection of Liberty and Twenty-second Streets. The Bank of America is to the right of the intersection. To the left is the former corporation court building and several city buildings can be seen on Twentieth Street near the left center. Catty-cornered from the Bank of America and at the intersection of Liberty and Twenty-second Streets is South Norfolk Loan office. This later became the Bank of Hampton Roads. *From the author's collection.*

In 1968, the members of Chesapeake Avenue Methodist Church were faced with having to build a new sanctuary. The fifty-year-old church was damaged beyond repair by termites. Judge Jerry G. Bray Jr. (left) and Dr. J.W. (Mike) Creef are seen here; these men and others met many times to plan and approve drawings of the new church building. *From the author's collection.*

THE 1970s–2005

A lot has happened since the merger of South Norfolk with Norfolk County in 1963. The early years after the merger saw South Norfolk acquire a lot of slums. Many families that had been the backbone of the City of South Norfolk moved to other parts of the new city. There was an influx of people who owed no allegiance to the area. Many brought with them the criminal way of life. Hopefully, through the efforts of several local organizations and new people in city government, there is a good chance that things will turn around.

In this section of the book I would like to include a few later photographs of the area and some of the annual events that the citizens support and enjoy.

1970s

This is a 1970s view of the triple-decker overpass on Bainbridge Boulevard at the Military Highway. The lower roadway is Bainbridge Boulevard looking north, the middle is a railroad track and the top is Military Highway. *From the author's collection.*

The South Norfolk all-stars of the Mustang League won the World Series in 1979. *Front row, left to right:* Donnie Sellers, Rodney Griffin, Greg Beck, Sylvester Hines and Terry Skinner; *second row:* James Harvey, Richard Lorenz, Scotty Shelton, Curt Dunlow, Tommy Mackley and Jeff Bradshaw; *third row:* Chuck Williams, Ben White, Leroy Mason and Pat O'Neal; *back row:* Bill Lorenz, Glenn Barker and Dennis Phelps. Sorry Ben, I couldn't remove the glasses. *Photo courtesy of Ben White and Jim Anglim.*

This ca. 1970s picture was taken at Lakeside Park on Holly Street in South Norfolk. This was probably the last time that the lake froze solid enough to skate on. *Photo courtesy of Bennie White Jr.*

1980s

In October 1982 the South Norfolk waterfront was still busy. The white building in the center of this photograph was a part of the Norfolk terminal of the Texas Oil Company. The vertical-rise bridge near the bottom right is the railroad bridge. After almost ninety years on the South Norfolk waterfront the Texas Oil Company closed in the latter 1990s. *Photo courtesy of Frankie Sweetwood.*

This 1987 photograph shows three of the houses in the South Norfolk Historic District. The house on the right was originally the home of William Lane, the one in the middle was the home of his brother J.T. (Tom) Lane and the house partly hidden by the trees was the home of E.M. Tilley. *From the author's collection.*

2000s

This is a recent photograph of the Lafarge cement plant at 100 Pratt Street in the Money Point section of South Norfolk and the Elizabeth River terminals. *From the author's collection.*

This picture was taken at the corner of Poindexter and Phillips Streets in February 2000 by Kathy Keeny, photographer for *Port Folio* magazine. *From the author's collection.*

This small house at 1414 Hoover Avenue across from Cascade Park was at one time the home of the Beacon Bible Class of the Chesapeake Avenue Methodist Church. It was around the latter 1950s that it was placed on a flat bed and transported to its present location. At that time the name of the street was Hawthorne Avenue. A few years after the merger with Norfolk County, the name was changed to Hoover Avenue. This picture was taken by Ellen Twine Old on April 2, 2000. *Photo courtesy of Ellen Twine Old.*

The City of South Norfolk built Cascade Park in 1934. At that time it was the finest athletic field in the Tidewater area. The playing field was used for both football and baseball and was the home of the South Norfolk Aces as well as the South Norfolk High School Tigers. This photograph was taken by Ellen Twine Old on April 14, 2000. *Photo courtesy of Ellen Twine Old.*

This picture, which was taken from Park Avenue, shows a part of Cascade Park as well as the southern end of Hoover Avenue. The photo was taken by Ellen Twine Old on April 11, 2000. *Photo courtesy of Ellen Twine Old.*

The members of the Chesapeake Museum enjoyed their annual Christmas celebration at the museum in December 2000. Whenever we had food an invitation was always extended to the firefighters from fire station number two. *From the author's collection.*

This picture, which was taken in December 2002, shows Ann Myers at the Chesapeake Museum where she is making preparations for the "CHIPS" cookie exchange. *From the author's collection.*

The telephone building in South Norfolk is behind the South Norfolk Baptist Church on Guerriere Street at the corner of Seaboard Avenue. I sold this property to the Chesapeake and Potomac Telephone Company in 1948. During my youth it was a nut grove where the neighborhood boys played football and baseball. This picture was taken October 8, 2002. *From the author's collection.*

This picture was taken on Saturday, October 4, 2003, at Lakeside Park. It shows several tents set up for the first arts and craft festival in the park. It was scheduled for late September but due to Hurricane Isabel the event had to be rescheduled. *From the author's collection.*

In the early 1900s there was a marsh at the corner of Bainbridge Boulevard and Holly Street. It extended from Bainbridge Boulevard over to Hull Street. This piece of property was among many that belonged to Frank L. Portlock Sr. Portlock had pilings driven and the land filled, after which he had a building constructed there. In the year 2004, almost one hundred years later, when the land was prepared for construction of the Dollar General store, these pilings were found and were as solid as the day they were driven. Actually the tops had to be cut off. The pilings can be seen in this photo that was taken on April 5, 2004. *From the author's collection.*

This photograph, which was taken in 2005, shows the tugboat *Night Hawk* pushing a barge loaded with sand. When this picture was snapped the tug was passing under the Jordan Bridge. To the left and straight ahead is what was at one time the Cargill plant. Perdue Farms now operates it. *From the author's collection.*

This is the third annual arts and crafts festival, which was held in Lakeside Park on Saturday, September 9, and Sunday, September 10, 2005. Each year it just keeps getting better. *From the author's collection.*

This group of men are members of the Old-Timers Club. When it was first organized there were approximately 150 members and they met at the Butterfield Stage on Park Avenue. Later the club held its monthly meetings at the Double Deuce on Bainbridge Boulevard at the corner of Portlock Road. It now meets at Smokin' Joe's on Bainbridge Boulevard near Barnes Road. The club has no agenda and no program. It's just a group of men who meet in South Norfolk, talk about the old days and enjoy a buffet at noon the first Monday of each month. We always welcome new members. This photo was taken March 7, 2005. *From the author's collection.*

BERKLEY—VILLAGE AND TOWN

Berkley, which is one of the oldest communities in Virginia, had its beginning when John Herbert received land grants along the Elizabeth River in 1664 and again in 1667. This land across from Norfolk is at that point where the Southern Branch meets the Eastern Branch of the Elizabeth River. Practically the entire section was, at one time, owned by the Herbert family and was known as Herbertsville. The Herberts were boat builders and ship captains and in 1728 Henry Herbert, a descendant of John Herbert, established a shipyard that remained in operation until 1828. Henry died in 1778, leaving operation of the business to other members of the family. Some of the ships produced at the yard saw service during the Revolutionary War, and also in the undeclared war with France that took place during the administration of President John Adams.

Several generations of the Herbert family built two large brick homes facing the Elizabeth River. In the 1840s, Enoch Herbert, who then owned the property, decided to go west. He gave part of his property to his daughter Lydia and, in 1846, sold the rest to Thomas Asbury Hardy.

Hardy was born in Bertie County, North Carolina, in 1800. When he was twenty-six, he moved to Norfolk and became successful as a cotton and fertilizer broker and was the owner of a basket and barrel factory. In 1831 he married Elizabeth Margaret Pierce, a native of Norfolk, and they lived in a brick house at the northeast corner of Granby and Market Streets. In later years, this corner became a part of downtown Norfolk and was the location of Smith and Welton's department store.

Thomas and Elizabeth Hardy had fourteen children, one of whom was Mary Pinkney, who was born on March 22, 1852. On May 19, 1875, she married Arthur MacArthur. They had three children, the youngest, Douglas, was born January 26, 1880. Douglas graduated from West Point in 1903 and spent most of his life in the U.S. Army. In World War II he became General of the Army and was the first five-star general.

When Colonel William Byrd II stopped on his way to North Carolina in 1728, he referred to the area as Powder Point because the Town of Norfolk kept a magazine there for the storage of gunpowder. Later the name was changed to Ferry Point because the Norfolk County ferry docked at the foot of what would become Chestnut Street. Still later in the eighteenth century, the name was again changed to Washington Point.

On December 20, 1787, the first marine hospital in the United States was erected at the foot of Chestnut Street. During the Civil War, it was used as a barracks for Confederate troops; by 1896, it housed the Berkley Military Institute. It was early in the twentieth century that Paul Garrett of Garrett & Company Winery acquired the old hospital, had it remodeled and used it for his family residence. It then became known as the Garrett mansion. During World War I, the building served as the Imperial Club, an entertainment spot for enlisted men. After standing for almost one hundred fifty years the grand old structure was torn down in 1933.

In 1789, the Virginia legislature chose Powder Point as the location for the next county courthouse. In 1801 the courthouse was moved to Portsmouth where it remained until the City of South Norfolk merged with Norfolk County in 1963, to form the City of Chesapeake.

According to tradition, a French nobleman by the name of Montalant first inhabited the residential section of Berkley that would later bear his name. As the story goes, he and some of his followers came to the area about 1790 to escape the French Revolution.

About 1846, Saint Helena, that land south of Washington Point, was sold to the United States government. This property was used as a naval training station. After World War II, the Norfolk Division of the College of William and Mary and the Virginia Polytechnic Institute used the abandoned barracks as classrooms.

Magnolia Cemetery came into being when three unknown soldiers were buried in a field. Later, others—including residents who were then soldiers of the Confederacy—were laid to rest in the Confederate Square section of the cemetery.

Berkley's beginning as a progressive community began after the Civil War, when Lycurgus Berkley began to develop the area as a town. The town's accessibility to the sea and the availability of raw materials brought a large number of investors from outside the area. In the late 1800s and early 1900s, lumber mills, box factories, knitting mills and shipyards began to spring up, and fortunes were made overnight. Several financial institutions were organized. In 1903, Paul Garrett opened a branch of Garrett & Company Winery in Berkley. Garrett operated the winery until Prohibition forced him to close in 1916.

On March 3, 1890, the Town of Berkley was created; it was short lived, as the City of Norfolk annexed it in 1906.

Berkley's period of prosperity, however, was only temporary. By World War I, the old village at the fork of the Elizabeth River's Eastern and Southern Branches went into decline. Prohibition had closed the Garrett winery; dwindling forests caused the box factories and lumber mills to leave. Well-to-do families moved across the river to Norfolk and rented out their large Berkley homes. The homes were divided into apartments and received very little upkeep. The tenants destroyed a large number of the beautiful old homes. Structures of historic significance were torn down. Commercial vessels increased in size, making it necessary for their owners to use shipyards that were located on deeper water; Saint Helena Naval Training Station was incorporated into Norfolk Naval Station. To add to all this, a fire in 1922 destroyed much of Berkley. A few of the old homes and churches still stand, but most of Berkley has given way to the wrecking ball.

Some improvements have begun to take place. New residences are beginning to pop up on some of the old streets. The area had been without a grocery store until recently, when Farm Fresh built a supermarket in Berkley. Prior to that the local citizens had to take a bus to Norfolk or South Norfolk to grocery shop. Someday maybe the community will regain at least part of what has been lost.

This is the Cummer Lumber Company on the Berkley waterfront as it appeared in 1895. *Courtesy of Sargeant Memorial Room, Norfolk Public Library, Norfolk, Virginia.*

Volunteers and later contracted fire companies provided early fire protection in Berkley. One such contractor was the Hope Fire Company. This early photograph, ca. 1910, shows the third precinct police station and the right side of the fire station at that time. Note the watering trough on the sidewalk. Horses pulled all the fire engines and other wagons at that time. *Courtesy of Sargeant Memorial Room, Norfolk Public Library, Norfolk, Virginia.*

In 1915, the Berkley Fire Department Engine Co. 8 was built on the south side of East Liberty Street near South Main Street. The horses were kept in stalls behind the lower level. The police department occupied the right side of the building. *Courtesy of Sargeant Memorial Room, Norfolk Public Library, Norfolk, Virginia.*

This photograph of Berkley Fire Station number 8 and the third police precinct was taken by H.C. Mann sometime between 1915 and 1922. The structure was of brick and stone and contained a tall brick lookout tower at the rear of the building. The streetcar tracks can be seen in front of the building on Liberty Street. *Courtesy of Sargeant Memorial Room, Norfolk Public Library, Norfolk, Virginia.*

About 1846, Saint Helena, that land south of Washington Point and directly across the Elizabeth River from the Gosport (later named Norfolk) Navy Yard, was sold to the U.S. government. The property was used as a naval training station. In later years the U.S. Coast Guard used a part of it. This picture of Camp Perry and the next four photographs of Saint Helena were taken in 1910. *Courtesy of Sargeant Memorial Room, Norfolk Public Library, Norfolk, Virginia.*

This was Camp Dewey at Saint Helena Naval Training Station in Berkley in 1910. *Courtesy of Sargeant Memorial Room, Norfolk Public Library, Norfolk, Virginia.*

The building with the Red Cross flag in front is the Naval Dispensary at Camp Dewey. Note the early ambulance beside the building. This 1910 picture was taken at Saint Helena Naval Training Station in Berkley. *Courtesy of Sargeant Memorial Room, Norfolk Public Library, Norfolk, Virginia.*

This part of Saint Helena Naval Training Station is Camp Farragut. *Courtesy of Sargeant Memorial Room, Norfolk Public Library, Norfolk, Virginia.*

Probably the most important part of any naval station is the mess hall. This one fed the men from Camp Perry and Camp Farragut at Saint Helena Naval Training Station in 1910. *Courtesy of Sargeant Memorial Room, Norfolk Public Library, Norfolk, Virginia.*

This large plant is the Berkley Ice Works as it appeared in 1910. All deliveries were made by horse and wagon. *Courtesy of Sargeant Memorial Room, Norfolk Public Library, Norfolk, Virginia.*

In colonial days this was known as the "street that leadeth down to the waterside." Later it was known as "Market Square." It was here that country people came with their poultry, eggs, butter and vegetables. Still later it was given the name "Commercial Place." In this very busy ca. 1910 photograph we see the docking place for the Berkley and Portsmouth ferries. Berkley is in the left background. *Courtesy of Sargeant Memorial Room, Norfolk Public Library, Norfolk, Virginia.*

In 1903, Paul Garrett opened a branch of Garrett & Company Winery in Berkley at the foot of Chestnut Street. This photograph shows the winery as it was in 1912. The large building in the right background was built in 1787 and was the first marine hospital in the United States. Eventually it was acquired by Paul Garrett who had it totally remodeled and used it for his family's residence. It then became known as the Garrett mansion. *Courtesy of Sargeant Memorial Room, Norfolk Public Library, Norfolk, Virginia.*

H.C. Mann took this ca. 1916 photograph shortly after the Berkley Bridge opened. The points of interest are, from left to right, Norfolk and Western Railroad Union Station, the Berkley Bridge and the Herbert/Hardy House. *Courtesy of Sargeant Memorial Room, Norfolk Public Library, Norfolk, Virginia.*

The Berkley Bridge that ran from South Main Street in Berkley to East Main Street in Norfolk was built in 1916. The Herbert/Hardy House can be seen to the left of the bridge near the upper right in this photograph, which was taken in 1917. Older southside residents will remember riding the streetcar across the bridge and paying a two-cent toll each way. Several toll collectors made their home in South Norfolk. *Courtesy of Sargeant Memorial Room, Norfolk Public Library, Norfolk, Virginia.*

On Thursday, April 13, 1922, the day before Good Friday, more than a third of Berkley was wiped out by fire. Some sources reported that the blaze started in one of the sheds at the abandoned Tunis Lumber Mill, when an illegal liquor still exploded. A large number of photographers, both amateur and professional, took many pictures during and after the fire. C.S. Borjes took this one and the one that follows. *Courtesy of Sargeant Memorial Room, Norfolk Public Library, Norfolk, Virginia.*

This photograph does not depict the aftermath of a World War II bombing raid. Actually C.S. Borjes took it after the Berkley fire in April 1922. *Courtesy of Sargeant Memorial Room, Norfolk Public Library, Norfolk, Virginia.*

This large house was built in 1787 at the foot of Chestnut Street and served as the first marine hospital in the United States. It was later remodeled and became the home of Paul Garrett and his family. This picture was taken in March 1933 when it was about 146 years old and was demolished soon after. The lovely old home can be seen here with the streetcar tracks running on the street beside it. *Courtesy of Sargeant Memorial Room, Norfolk Public Library, Norfolk, Virginia.*

The intersection of Liberty and Thirteenth Streets was a short distance from the dividing line between South Norfolk and Berkley. This picture was taken on Easter Sunday, April 21, 1946. *Courtesy of Sargeant Memorial Room, Norfolk Public Library, Norfolk, Virginia.*

The Berkley Branch Library was established in this small house at the corner of Patrick and South Main Streets on April 21, 1921. Miss Lee Dudley was the librarian. *Courtesy of Sargeant Memorial Room, Norfolk Public Library, Norfolk, Virginia.*

This picture, which was taken in 1951, is from the Emmerson collection. This large unusual house is located at the corner of Cross and Patrick Streets. Note the iron fence around the front of the house. *Courtesy of Sargeant Memorial Room, Norfolk Public Library, Norfolk, Virginia.*

In 1910, this was the Merchant and Planters Bank. When this picture was taken on April 24, 1985, its name was Sovran Bank. This branch no longer exists. *Courtesy of Sargeant Memorial Room, Norfolk Public Library, Norfolk, Virginia.*

OTHER BOOKS BY THE AUTHOR

Dear Old Golden Rule Days. Privately printed, 2003.

History of South Norfolk: 1661–1963, Volumes I and II. Privately printed, 1996.

Images of America: Norfolk County. Charleston, SC: Arcadia Publishing, 2000.

Images of America: South Norfolk. Charleston, SC: Arcadia Publishing, 1999.

Making of America: Chesapeake, Virginia. Charleston, SC: Arcadia Publishing, 2002.

South Norfolk, Virginia, 1661–2005: A Definitive History, Volumes I and II. Charleston, SC: The History Press, 2005.

Then & Now: South Norfolk. Charleston, SC: Arcadia Publishing, 2003.

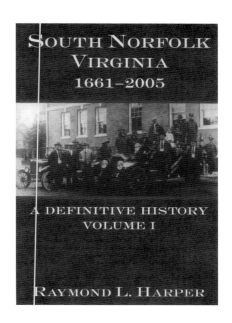

SOUTH NORFOLK,
VIRGINIA
1661–2005
A DEFINITIVE HISTORY
VOLUME I
1-59629-065-X
224 PP. • $24.99

South Norfolk native and local historian Raymond Harper honors the dynamic history of the city by focusing not only on the founding fathers and early industries that shaped the area, but upon the lives of everyday families and individuals as well.

SOUTH NORFOLK,
VIRGINIA
1661–2005
A DEFINITIVE HISTORY
VOLUME II
1-59629-066-8
224 PP. • $24.99

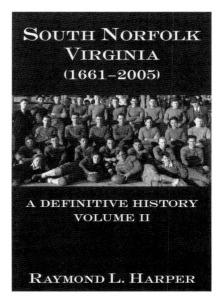